Congressional
Research Service
Informing the legislative debate since 1914 _____

Reserve Component Personnel Issues: Questions and Answers

Lawrence Kapp
Specialist in Military Manpower Policy

Barbara Salazar Torreon
Information Research Specialist

June 13, 2014

Congressional Research Service

7-5700

www.crs.gov

RL30802

Summary

The strength of the nation's Armed Forces, including the reserve components, has historically been an area of keen interest to Congress. The increasing use of the reserves since the end of the Cold War has led to greater congressional interest in various issues that bear on the vitality of the reserve components, such as funding, equipment, and personnel policy. This report is designed to provide an overview of key reserve component personnel issues.

The term "Reserve Component" refers collectively to the seven individual reserve components of the Armed Forces: the Army National Guard of the United States, the Army Reserve, the Navy Reserve, the Marine Corps Reserve, the Air National Guard of the United States, the Air Force Reserve, and the Coast Guard Reserve. The purpose of these seven reserve components, as codified in law at 10 U.S.C. 10102, is to "provide trained units and qualified persons available for active duty in the armed forces, in time of war or national emergency, and at such other times as the national security may require, to fill the needs of the armed forces whenever more units and persons are needed than are in the regular components."

During the Cold War era, the reserve components were a manpower pool that was rarely tapped. From 1945 to 1989, reservists were involuntarily activated by the federal government four times, an average of less than once per decade. Since the end of the Cold War, the nation has relied more heavily on the reserve components. Reservists have been involuntarily activated for contingency operations by the federal government six times since 1990, an average of once every four years, including large-scale mobilizations for the Persian Gulf War (1990-1991) and in the aftermath of the September 11 terrorist attacks (2001-present). Additionally, starting in FY2014, reservists began to be involuntarily activated under a new authority for "pre-planned" missions in support of Combatant Commanders.

This report provides insight to reserve component personnel issues through a series of questions and answers which address:

- How reserve component personnel are organized (questions 2 and 4);

- How many people are in each of the different categories of the reserve component (question 3);

- How reserve component personnel have been and may be used (questions 1, 5, 6, 7, 9, and 11);

- How reserve component personnel are compensated (questions 8 and 10);

- The types of legal protections that exist for reserve component personnel (question 12); and

- Recent changes in reserve component pay and benefits made by Congress (question 13).

Contents

Tables

Contacts

1. What Is the Reserve Component? What Is Its Role?

The term "Reserve Component" (RC) refers collectively to the seven individual reserve components of the Armed Forces: the Army National Guard of the United States, the Army Reserve, the Navy Reserve,[1] the Marine Corps Reserve, the Air National Guard of the United States, the Air Force Reserve, and the Coast Guard Reserve. The purpose of these seven reserve components, as codified in law, is to "provide trained units and qualified persons available for active duty in the armed forces, in time of war or national emergency, and at such other times as the national security may require, to fill the needs of the armed forces whenever more units and persons are needed than are in the regular components."[2] The Army National Guard and the Air National Guard also have a state role: In addition to the role of providing trained units and personnel to the Armed Forces of the United States, they also assist the states in responding to various emergencies, such as disasters and civil disorders. (For more information on the difference between the National Guard and other reserve components, see "5. What Is the Difference Between the "Reserves" and the "National Guard"?" and "11. Are There Other Ways in Which Members of the National Guard Can Be Activated?")

2. What Are the Different Categories of Reservists?

All reservists, whether they are in the Reserves or the National Guard,[3] are assigned to one of three major reserve categories: the Ready Reserve, the Standby Reserve, or the Retired Reserve. Reservists who are assigned to the Ready Reserve are further assigned to one of its three sub-components: the Selected Reserve, the Individual Ready Reserve (IRR), or the Inactive National Guard (ING). The differences between each of these categories are explained below.

The Ready Reserve

The Ready Reserve is the primary manpower pool of the reserve components. Members of the Ready Reserve will usually be called to active duty before members of the Standby Reserve[4] or

---

[1] The National Defense Authorization Act for FY2006 (P.L. 109-163, Section 515) changed the name of the Naval Reserve to the Navy Reserve.

[2] 10 U.S.C. 10102. The language was changed by P.L. 108-375, the Ronald W. Reagan National Defense Authorization Act for FY2005. Prior to this change, the language was as follows: "The purpose of each reserve component is to provide trained units and qualified persons available for active duty in the armed forces, in time of war or national emergency, and at such other times as the national security may require, to fill the needs of the armed forces whenever, during and after the period needed to procure and train additional units and qualified persons to achieve the planned mobilization, more units and persons are needed than are in the regular components." The change in statutory language, as explained in a House Armed Services Committee report, would "clarify that the purpose of the reserve components is to provide trained units and qualified personnel not just as the result of involuntary mobilizations but whenever more units and persons are needed than are in the active component. The revision recommended by this section more accurately reflects recent and future employments of the reserve components." H.Rept. 108-491, p. 316.

[3] For a discussion of the distinction between the Reserves and the National Guard, see questions 5 and 11.

[4] Units and members of the Standby Reserve may be involuntarily ordered to active duty under the provisions of 10 U.S.C. 12301(a) [see Question 9, Full Mobilization, for a description of this authority]; however, 10 U.S.C. 12306(b) specifies that "No unit in the Standby Reserve organized to serve as a unit or any member thereof may be ordered to active duty under Section 12301(a) of this title, unless the Secretary concerned, with the approval of the Secretary of (continued...)

---

the Retired Reserve. The Ready Reserve is made up of the Selected Reserve, the Individual Ready Reserve, and the Inactive National Guard, each of which is described below.

The Selected Reserve

The Selected Reserve contains those units and individuals within the Ready Reserve designated as so essential to initial wartime missions that they have priority over all other Reserves.[5] Members of the Selected Reserve are generally required to perform one weekend of training each month ("inactive duty for training" or IDT, also known colloquially as "weekend drill") and two weeks of training each year ("annual training" or AT, sometimes known colloquially as "summer camp") for which they receive pay and benefits. Some members of the Selected Reserve perform considerably more military duty than this, while others may only be required to perform the two weeks of annual training each year or other combinations of time.[6] Members of the Selected Reserve can be involuntarily ordered to active duty under each of the main activation authorities. (See "9. How Are Reservists Called to Active Duty by the Federal Government? How Often Does this Happen? After Activation, How Long Can They Be Required to Serve on Active Duty?" for more information on activation authorities.)

The Individual Ready Reserve

The Individual Ready Reserve (IRR) is a manpower pool of individuals who have already received military training, either in the Active Component or in the Selected Reserve.[7] Members of the IRR may be required to perform regular training,[8] although DOD has not implemented such a requirement since the 1950s. Members of the IRR can volunteer for training or active duty assignments, and they can also be involuntarily ordered to active duty under a Full Mobilization, Partial Mobilization, or a Disaster Response Activation. There is also a category of the IRR that can be activated during a Presidential Reserve Call-up, but at present there is no one assigned to this category. (See "9. How Are Reservists Called to Active Duty by the Federal Government? How Often Does this Happen? After Activation, How Long Can They Be Required to Serve on Active Duty?" for more information on mobilization authorities.) There is no IRR in the Army National Guard or the Air National Guard, although there is an analogous category in the Army National Guard known as the Inactive National Guard (see "The Inactive National Guard," immediately below).

(...continued)

Defense in the case of a Secretary of a military department, determines that there are not enough of the required kinds of units in the Ready Reserve that are readily available." A similar provision applies to members of the Standby Reserve not assigned to a unit.

[5] Department of Defense Instruction 1215.06, *Uniform Reserve, Training and Retirement Categories*, February 7, 2007 (Incorporating Change 2, December 24, 2008), 29, at http://www.dtic.mil/whs/directives/corres/pdf/121506p.pdf

[6] For example, members of the Selected Reserve often volunteer to perform extra duty, while some members of the Individual Mobilization Augmentee (IMA) program may only perform two weeks of training per year. Other members of the IMA program may be required to perform IDT training as well, but typically perform it during weekdays rather than on weekends.

[7] Department of Defense Instruction 1215.06, 32, at http://www.dtic.mil/whs/directives/corres/pdf/121506p.pdf

[8] 10 U.S.C. §10147.

The Inactive National Guard

The Inactive National Guard (ING) is made up of those members of the Army National Guard who are in an inactive status (currently there is no ING for the Air National Guard). They are not required to participate in training as are members of the Selected Reserve; however, they are attached to a specific National Guard unit and are required to meet with the unit once a year.[9] Members of the ING can be involuntarily ordered to active duty if the unit they are attached to is activated under a Partial Mobilization, or a Full Mobilization. They are not subject to activation under a Presidential Reserve Call Up.[10] (See "9. How Are Reservists Called to Active Duty by the Federal Government? How Often Does this Happen? After Activation, How Long Can They Be Required to Serve on Active Duty?" for more information on activation authorities.) The ING is, for practical purposes, the National Guard equivalent of the IRR.

The Standby Reserve

The Standby Reserve contains those individuals who have a temporary disability or hardship and those who hold key defense related positions in their civilian jobs.[11] While in the Standby Reserve, reservists are not required to participate in military training and are subject to involuntary activation only in the case of a Full Mobilization. (See "9. How Are Reservists Called to Active Duty by the Federal Government? How Often Does this Happen? After Activation, How Long Can They Be Required to Serve on Active Duty?" for more information on activation authorities.)

The Retired Reserve

The Retired Reserve includes (1) Reserve officers and enlisted personnel who are receiving retired pay as a result of their reserve and/or active service; and (2) Reserve officers and enlisted personnel who transfer into the Retired Reserve after qualifying for reserve retirement, but before becoming eligible to receive retired pay (which normally occurs at age 60). Regular officers and enlisted personnel who are receiving retired pay are not included in the Retired Reserve. Members of the Retired Reserve may be involuntarily ordered to active duty in the event of a Full Mobilization, and some members of the Retired Reserve may be ordered to active duty in the event of a recall of retirees. (See "9. How Are Reservists Called to Active Duty by the Federal Government? How Often Does this Happen? After Activation, How Long Can They Be Required to Serve on Active Duty?" for more information on activation authorities.)

---

[9] Department of Defense Instruction 1215.06, 33.

[10] Department of Defense Directive 1235.13, *Management of the Individual Ready Reserve and the Inactive National Guard*, July 16, 2005, p 2.

[11] Department of Defense Instruction 1215.06, 33.

3. How Many People Are in the Reserve Components?

As of September 30, 2013, the total reported personnel strength of the Ready Reserve was 1,102,419. This figure is broken down by service and category of reservist in **Table 1**. In addition, there were another 13,640 members of the Standby Reserve and 745,235 members of the Retired Reserve, although these categories of reservists are much less likely to be mobilized than Ready Reservists.[12] Additionally, a substantial percentage of the Retired Reserve would likely be unable to mobilize due to age and fitness.

It is worth noting that the personnel strength of the Selected Reserve for the Army National Guard has been near or above its authorized level for the past seven years, capping a turnaround from the middle of the past decade when it fell significantly below its authorized level. From the end of FY2003 to the end of FY2005, the Army National Guard's Selected Reserve strength dropped from 351,089 to 333,177. By the end of FY2007 this had increased to 352,707 (a figure slightly above its FY2007 authorized end-strength of 350,000), and by the end of FY2008 it had increased to 360,351 (nearly 3% above its FY2008 authorized end-strength of 351,300). Congress increased the Army National Guard's authorized end-strength to 358,200 in FY2010, and its actual strength in FY2010-FY2013 has stayed very close to that higher level. Congress reduced the Army National Guard's authorized end strength to 354,200 for FY2014.

A similar turnaround in personnel strength also occurred in the Army Reserve, although a reversal of this trend has occurred in recent years. From the end of FY2003 to the end of FY2005, the Army Reserve's Selected Reserve strength dropped from 211,890 to 189,005, significantly below its authorized end-strength of 205,000. This was followed by two years in which the decline was halted, but little progress was made towards restoring the lost strength. However, in FY2008 the Army Reserve showed substantial growth, increasing its end-strength by over 7,000 and achieving 96% of its authorized end-strength. The Army Reserve maintained a strength level very near its authorized end-strength in FY2009-FY2011. However, it dropped to 200,910 at the end of FY2012, about 2% below its authorized end-strength, and to 198,209 at the end of FY2013, about 3.5% below its authorized end-strength in FY2013. In FY2014, this decline appears to be continuing, with Army Reserve strength at 196,251 as of April 2014. These declines are occuring in a relatively strong recruiting environment and amidst a major reduction in active Army strength which provides a fairly large pool of potential prior-service recruits.

Personnel strength in the Selected Reserve of the Navy Reserve has declined for the past ten years, but this decline appears to be consistent with the Navy's plans to realign the Navy Reserve with active component requirements and eliminate unneeded structure.[13] The Selected Reserve of

---

[12] Figures do not included Standby Reserve or Retired Reserve for Coast Guard.

[13] The Navy Reserve had an actual Selected Reserve strength of 88,156 at the end of FY2003. That level has decreased each year since, to an actual strength of 62,444 at the end of FY2013. The reduction in Navy Reserve strength was initiated by a 2003 review of Navy Reserve manpower requirements in light of the changing military environment and military requirements. This review, which recommended reducing the Navy Reserve by roughly 16,000 Selected Reserve positions (to about 70,000 Selected Reserve positions by 2011) was approved by the Chief of Naval Operations in August 2004. See U.S. Government Accountability Office, *Force Structure: Assessments of Navy Reserve Manpower Requirements Need to Consider Most Cost-effective Mix of Active and Reserve Manpower to Meet Mission Needs*, GAO-06-125, October 2005, pp. 5-6, http://www.gao.gov/new.items/d06125.pdf. According to subsequent congressional testimony by Navy leaders, it appears that additional strength reductions were implemented (continued...)

---

the Air Force Reserve also saw a planned reduction in its personnel strength in the FY2006-FY2008 timeframe, but has since restored about 40% of those cuts.[14]

Table 1. Personnel Strength of the Ready Reserve as of September 2013

	Selected Reserve	Individual Ready Reserve/ Inactive National Guard	Total Ready Reserve
Army National Guard	357,735	2,436	360,171
Army Reserve	198,209	106,012	304,221
Navy Reserve	62,444	47,294	109,738
Marine Corps Reserve	39,501	68,715	108,216
Air National Guard	105,708	0	105,708
Air Force Reserve	70,913	33,964	104,877
Coast Guard Reserve	8,000	1,488	9,488
Total	**842,510**	**259,909**	**1,102,419**

Source: Data provided by the Department of Defense.

4. What Does "Full-time Support" Mean? What Are the Different Categories of Full-time Support for the Reserve Components?

Reserve units are primarily filled by "traditional" reservists: members of the Selected Reserve who are usually required to work one weekend a month and two weeks a year. However, most reserve units are also staffed by one or more full-time civilian and/or military employees. These employees, known as full-time support (FTS) personnel, are "assigned to organize; administer; instruct; recruit and train; maintain supplies, equipment and aircraft; and perform other functions

---

(...continued)

as part of an ongoing force structure review process to align reserve capabilities with active component requirements. See prepared statement of Vice Admiral John C. Harvey, Chief of Naval Personnel, before the Senate Armed Services Personnel Subcommittee, February 27, 2008, p. 92, http://www.gpo.gov/fdsys/pkg/CHRG-110shrg42634/pdf/CHRG-110shrg42634.pdf .

[14] The Air Force Reserve had a strength of 75,802 at the end of FY2005. That level decreased to a strength of 67,565 by the end of FY2008, and then increased to a strength of 70,913 by the end of FY2013. Air Force budget documents variously characterize the reductions which began in FY2006 as related to active/reserve rebalancing, recapitalization efforts, and active-reserve integration. See Air Force Reserve Budget Estimates (Reserve Personnel, Air Force) for FY2006 (p. 6), FY2007 (p. 8), FY2008 (p. 7), and FY2009 (p. 8), available at http://www.saffm hq.af mil/shared/media/document/AFD-080204-074.pdf. The increase which began in FY2009 was tied to the Department of Defense decision to halt the drawdown of active duty Air Force end strength at 330,000 personnel (rather than the planned 322,000). See Air Force Reserve Fiscal Year 2011 Budget Estimates, February 2010, p. 7, available at http://www.saffm hq.af mil/shared/media/document/AFD-100127-158.pdf . See also Sam Lagrone, *Air Force Times*, "Air Force Reserve Plans to Add 4,000 Airmen," February 3, 2009, available at http://www.airforcetimes.com/article/20090203/NEWS/902030337/Air-Force-Reserve-plans-add-4-000-airmen.

---

required on a daily basis in the execution of operational missions and readiness preparations as authorized in Title 5, Title 10, and Title 32.... "[15]

There are five types of FTS personnel: Active Guard & Reserve, Military Technician, Non-Dual Status Technician, Active Component, and Civilian. The distinctions between each of these categories are outlined below. The mix of FTS personnel in each of the reserve components (RC) is intended "to optimize consistency and stability for each RC to achieve its assigned missions."[16] **Table 2** provides a summary of FTS personnel strength, broken down by service and category, as of September 30, 2013.

Active Guard and Reserve

Active Guard and Reserve (AGR) personnel are members of a Reserve Component who are placed on active duty or full-time National Guard duty orders for a period of 180 consecutive days or more for the purpose of "organizing, administering, recruiting, instructing, or training the reserve components."[17] They may also perform certain operational support duties, and certain duties related to defense against weapons of mass destruction, as well as provide training to active component personnel, DOD contractors, DOD civilians, and foreign military personnel.[18] Although they are serving full-time, AGR personnel are still considered members of the Selected Reserve. They are usually required to attend weekend drills and annual training with the reserve unit to which they are assigned.

Depending on their branch of service, AGR personnel are referred to by different names. In the Army National Guard, Army Reserve, Air National Guard, and Air Force Reserve, they are simply referred to as AGRs, an acronym for Active Guard and Reserve. In the Navy Reserve they are referred to as TARs, an acronym for Training and Administration of Reserves. In the Coast Guard Reserve, they are referred to as RPAs, an acronym for Reserve Program Administrators. In the Marine Corps Reserve, they are known as Marine Corps Active Reserves or ARs.

Military Technicians

Military technicians (MTs) are federal civilian employees who provide support to reserve units, either in the administration and training of reserve component units, or by maintaining and repairing reserve component equipment and supplies.[19] Some MTs may also perform certain operational support duties and provide training to active component personnel, DOD contractors, DOD civilians, and foreign military personnel.[20] Unlike regular civilian employees, MTs are generally required to maintain membership in the Selected Reserve as a condition of their employment. They are sometimes referred to as "dual-status military technicians," reflecting their

---

[15] Department of Defense Instruction (DODI) 1205.18, "Full Time Support (FTS) to the Reserve Components," May 4, 2007, enclosure 2, paragraph E2.4, at http://www.dtic.mil/whs/directives/corres/pdf/120518p.pdf.

[16] DODI 1205.18, paragraph 4.2, at http://www.dtic.mil/whs/directives/corres/pdf/120518p.pdf .

[17] 10 U.S.C. §101(d)(6)(A). See also DODI 1205.18, 8.

[18] 10 U.S.C. §12310. AGR personnel can also serve "at headquarters responsible for reserve affairs, to participate in preparing and administering the policies and regulations affecting those reserve components." 10 U.S.C. §10211. See also DODI 1205.18, 8.

[19] 10 U.S.C. §10216. See also DODI 1205.18, 8.

[20] 10 U.S.C. §10216(a)(3)(C).

status as both federal civilian employees and military reservists.[21] They are required to attend weekend drills and annual training with their reserve unit, which is usually the same unit they work for as civilians during the weekday. Military technicians can be involuntarily ordered to active duty in the same way as other members of the Selected Reserve (see "2. What Are the Different Categories of Reservists?"). There are no MTs in the Navy Reserve, the Marine Corps Reserve, or the Coast Guard Reserve.

Non-Dual Status Technicians

Non-dual status technicians (NDSTs) are civilian employees of the military departments serving in military technician positions. They are referred to as "non-dual-status technicians" because they are not members of the Selected Reserve and, hence, do not have a dual military/civilian status like MTs.[22] NDSTs perform the same functions as MTs, but cannot be ordered to active duty as they do not have a military status. There are no NDSTs in the Navy Reserve, the Marine Corps Reserve, or the Coast Guard Reserve, and very few in the Air Force Reserve.

Active Component

Active Component (AC) personnel are active-duty members of the military who "are assigned or attached to Reserve component organizations or units by their respective Service to provide advice, liaison, management, administration, training, and support."[23] Although they are formally members of the Active Component, not the Reserve Component, AC personnel may deploy with the reserve unit they are assigned to if the unit is mobilized.

Civilians

Civilians are federal civil service employees who "provide administration, training, maintenance, and recruiting support to the Reserve components."[24] They are not required to hold membership in the Selected Reserve as a condition of their employment, although some do so voluntarily. Unless they are members of the reserve components, they cannot be involuntarily ordered to active duty.

---

[21] They are referred to as "military technicians (dual status)" in statute. See 10 U.S.C. §10216.

[22] 10 U.S.C. §10217. For more information on MTs and NDSTs, see CRS Report RL30487, *Military Technicians: The Issue of Mandatory Retirement for Non- Dual-Status Technicians*, by Lawrence Kapp.

[23] DODI 1205.18, 8.

[24] DODI 1205.18, 8.

Table 2. Reserve Component Full Time Support Personnel as of September 30, 2013

	Active Guard and Reserve	Technician[a]	Active Component	Civilian	Total
Army National Guard	31,111	27,393	184	785	59,473
Army Reserve	16,372	9,040	68	3,060	28,540
Navy Reserve	10,143	0	1,948	782	12,8732,873
Marine Corps Reserve	2,244	0	3,778	293	6,315
Air National Guard	14,557	22,568	208	208	37,541
Air Force Reserve	2,813	8,992	521	3,865	16,191
Total	**77,24077,240**	**67,99367,993**	**6,707**	**8,993**	**160,933**

Source: Data provided by the Department of Defense

a.   Includes Dual Status and Non-Dual-Status Technicians

5. What Is the Difference Between the "Reserves" and the "National Guard"?

Although the term "reserves" is often used as a generic term to refer to all members of the seven individual reserve components, there is an important distinction between the five reserve components which are purely federal entities (the Army Reserve, Navy Reserve, Marine Corps Reserve, Air Force Reserve, and Coast Guard Reserve) and the two reserve components which are both federal and state entities (the Army National Guard and the Air National Guard). In this context, the five purely federal reserve components are sometimes referred to collectively as the Reserves, while the dual federal/state reserve components are referred to collectively as the National Guard.

The Reserves are of comparatively recent origin, having all been established in the 20th century. They were organized under Congress's constitutional authority "to raise and support Armies" and "to provide and maintain a Navy."[25] The National Guard has a much longer historical pedigree. It is descended from the colonial-era militias[26] which existed prior to the adoption of the Constitution. The Constitution does, however, contain provisions that recognize the existence of the militia and that give the federal government a certain amount of control over it.[27]

---

[25] U.S. Constitution, Article 1, Section 8, clauses 12 and 13.

[26] The colonial militia, which was derived from a longstanding English tradition and which required every able bodied free male (though Native Americans and free blacks were frequently excluded) to participate in the common defense of his town or locality, was the principal institution of colonial military power. Gradually, as the colonial population grew and military threats waned, a distinction arose between the unorganized militia (those members of the militia who were potentially liable for military service but who did not actively participate in military training) and the organized militia (those members of the militia who regularly trained for war and who responded first to military threats). Today, the U.S. Code still recognizes the militia as consisting of "all able-bodied males at least 17 years of age and ... under 45 years of age who are, or who have made a declaration of intention to become, citizens of the United States and of female citizens of the United States who are members of the National Guard." (10 U.S.C. 311) This provision of the law further divides the militia into the organized and the unorganized militia, and declares the National Guard and the Naval Militia to be the organized militia. At present New York, Ohio, and South Carolina have active Naval Militias.

[27] See U.S. Constitution, Article I, Section 8, clauses 15 and 16, and Article II, Section 2, clause 1.

Unlike the Reserves, which are exclusively federal organizations, the National Guard is usually both a state and a federal organization. The National Guard of the United States is made up of 54 separate National Guard organizations: one for each state, and one for Puerto Rico, Guam, the U.S. Virgin Islands, and the District of Columbia. While the District of Columbia National Guard is an exclusively federal organization and operates under federal control at all times, the other 53 National Guards operate as state or territorial organizations most of the time. In this capacity, each of these 53 organizations is identified by its state or territorial name (e.g., the California National Guard or the Puerto Rico National Guard), and is controlled by its respective governor. Due to their dual federal and state role, National Guardsmen can be called to duty in several different ways (see "9. How Are Reservists Called to Active Duty by the Federal Government? How Often Does this Happen? After Activation, How Long Can They Be Required to Serve on Active Duty?" and "11. Are There Other Ways in Which Members of the National Guard Can Be Activated?") and the mode of activation has important implications for the pay, benefits, and legal protections they receive (see "10. What Type of Pay, Benefits, and Legal Protections Are Provided to Reservists Mobilized for Operations Noble Eagle and Enduring Freedom?" and "12. What Type of Legal Protections Do Reservists Have When They Are Serving on Active Duty? What Reemployment Rights Do Reservists Have after Being Released from Active Duty?").

6. How Has the Role of the Reserve Components Changed in Recent Years?

In 2000, Charles Cragin, a former Assistant Secretary of Defense for Reserve Affairs, summed up the changing role of the reserve components in the following words: "The role of our Reserve forces is changing in the United States. We have seen their traditional role, which was to serve as manpower replacements in the event of some cataclysmic crisis, utterly transformed. They are no longer serving as the force of last resort, but as vital contributors on a day-to-day basis around the world."[28] His comments, well supported by historical data at the time he made them, became even more apt given the large reserve mobilization that has occurred since the September 11th terrorist attack on the United States.

During the Cold War era, the reserve components were a manpower pool that was rarely tapped. From 1945 to 1989, reservists were involuntarily activated for federal service[29] four times, an average of less than once per decade. These activations occurred only during wartime and national emergencies: the Korean War (1950-1953; 857,877 reservists involuntarily activated), the Berlin Crisis (1961-1962; 148,034 reservists involuntarily activated), the Cuban Missile Crisis (1962; 14,200 reservists involuntarily activated), and the Vietnam War/*U.S.S. Pueblo* Crisis (1968-1969; 37,643 reservists involuntarily activated).

The nation has relied more heavily on the reserve components since the end of the Cold War. Reservists have been involuntarily activated for federal service six times over the past 23 years.

---

[28] Charles L. Cragin, Assistant Secretary of Defense for Reserve Affairs, remarks printed in *The Officer*, September 2000, 34.

[29] This category excludes those who served on active duty under voluntary orders or annual training order and excludes members of the National Guard serving in a state status (see question 11). Additionally, with the exception of those mobilized in response to the terrorist attacks of September 11, 2001, it excludes involuntary activations of reservists for domestic reasons, such as responding to civic disorders.

Some of these activations have been directly related to war or armed conflict: for example, the Persian Gulf War (1990-1991; 238,729 reservists involuntarily activated), the low-intensity conflict with Iraq[30] (1998-2003; 6,108 reservists involuntarily activated), and military operations in the aftermath of the September 11th terrorist attacks which included Operations Noble Eagle, Enduring Freedom and Iraqi Freedom/New Dawn[31] (2001-present; 896,815 reservists involuntarily *and voluntarily* activated as of May 27, 2014).[32] Other activations have been in support of missions that were primarily peacekeeping and nation-building, such as the intervention in Haiti (1994-1996; 6,250 reservists involuntarily activated) and the Bosnian peacekeeping mission (1995-2004; 31,553 reservists involuntarily activated).[33] The ongoing Kosovo mission (1999-present; 11,485 reservists involuntarily activated through 2003; no available data since then) has been a combination of armed conflict and peacekeeping.[34]

---

[30] In the aftermath of the 1991 Persian Gulf War, the United States maintained a substantial military presence in the region in order to enforce the terms of the cease-fire agreements. The United States used this military force to compel Iraqi compliance with the terms of the cease fire agreements on a number of occasions. One of the most significant U.S. confrontations with Iraq began in late 1997, in response to Iraqi interference in the conduct of U.N. weapons inspections. As tensions with Iraq mounted, the United States began to build up its forces in the Gulf region. Subsequently, a nearly constant low-intensity air war took place in and over Iraq: Iraqi anti-aircraft weapons fired on U.S. and allied aircraft; the allies responded by bombarding these and other military targets. On February 24, 1998, President Clinton ordered a Presidential Reserve Call-up (which is the activation of reservists under Title 10, Section 12304 of the United States Code; for more information on this authority, see Question 9). The first reservists called under this authority entered active duty on March 1, 1998. This low-intensity conflict with Iraq changed to a high-intensity conflict on March 20, 2003, with the commencement of Operation Iraqi Freedom. On May 1, 2003, all operations associated with the low-intensity conflict—such as Operation Northern Watch and Operation Southern Watch—became part of Operation Iraqi Freedom. Since then, reservists involuntarily activated for operations related to Iraq have been ordered to active duty under the post-September 11, 2001, Partial Mobilization (for more information on mobilization authorities, see Question 9).

[31] Operation Noble Eagle is the name given to military operations related to homeland security and support to federal, state, and local agencies in the wake of the September 11 attacks. Operation Enduring Freedom includes ongoing operations in Afghanistan, operations against terrorists in other countries, and training assistance to foreign militaries which are conducting operations against terrorists. Operation Iraqi Freedom/New Dawn included both the invasion of Iraq and the subsequent counterinsurgency and rebuilding operations. The Iraq mission officially ended on December 15, 2011. Donna Miles, *American Forces Press Service*, "Panetta, Dempsey Mark End of Iraq Mission," http://www.army mil/article/70932/ .

[32] On June 10, 2008, the Department of Defense changed their methodology for reporting reserve activations. Prior to that date, the report was based only on involuntary mobilizations under 10 U.S.C. 12302. Additionally, the old report counted the total number of involuntary mobilization actions rather than the total number of individuals mobilized. Thus, reservists who had been mobilized twice were counted twice. Since that date, the report has been modified to include those who have been activated voluntarily under 10 U.S.C. 12301(d) and those reservists who have been activated involuntarily under 10 U.S.C. 12302 or 10 U.S.C. 12304, and retirees who have been recalled under 10 U.S.C. 688. Additionally, the report is based on Social Security Number, so that an individual who was activated twice is only counted once. Between September 11, 2001, and May 27, 2014, a total of 896,815 reservists (which includes the National Guard) have served under voluntary or involuntary federal orders for ONE, OEF, and OIF/OND. Of these, 38,489 were serving on active duty on May 27, 2014, while 858,326 had completed their tours and been released from active duty. Source: Department of Defense reserve component activation data, available here: http://www.defense.gov/documents/27-May-2014.pdf .

[33] On December 1, 2004, the last U.S. peacekeeping troops left Bosnia, as NATO handed over the stabilization mission to the European Union. However, a few hundred U.S. military personnel remain in Bosnia. Jim Garmone, *American Forces Press Service*, "U.S. Peacekeepers Finish Bosnia Mission, Case Colors," December 1, 2004. The remaining few American military personnel in Bosnia may include some reservists mobilized under the authority of the Partial Mobilization for ONE/OEF/OIF. Those figures were not available from DOD.

[34] In 2003, DOD stopped using the Presidential Reserve Callup authority that had been used since 1999 to activate reservists for Kosovo, and instead began using the broader Partial Mobilization authority used for ONE/OEF/OIF; starting in 2014, the Army began activating reservists for Kosovo under the Combatant Command Support Authority (10 USC 12301b), although it is unclear whether or not all reservists serving in Kosovo are now activated under (continued...)

It is important to point out that—except for Operations Noble Eagle, Enduring Freedom, and Iraqi Freedom/New Dawn—this tally of activations refers only to instances where reservists were involuntarily ordered into active federal service. It does not encompass the many instances where reservists have served on active duty under voluntary orders or annual training orders or, for members of the National Guard, service under state authority (see "11. Are There Other Ways in Which Members of the National Guard Can Be Activated?" for more information on "state active duty" and duty under Title 32 of the U.S. Code).

Data from the Office of the Assistant Secretary of Defense for Reserve Affairs (OASD/RA) sheds more light on the growing contribution of reservists to federal missions. According to OASD/RA, reservists contributed about 1 million "man-days" per year to their respective services between fiscal years 1986 and 1989. This contribution increased since then to the point where reservists contributed about 13 million days of work per year between fiscal years 1996 and 2001. With the large mobilization of reservists in support of Operations Noble Eagle, Enduring Freedom, and Iraqi Freedom/New Dawn, reservists contributed about 41.3 million days of work in FY2002 to a peak of 68.3 million days in FY2005. This metric dropped to 25.8 million days by FY2012, but it still represents a vastly higher level of activity than typically occurred in the Cold War era.[35] The continuing mobilization of reservists to participate in these operations, probably for some years to come, lends further support to the idea that the Reserve Component has been transformed from a "force of last resort" in the Cold War era into an integrated part of the military services in the post-Cold War era; this process has also been referred to as the transformation of the reserve component from a "strategic reserve" to an "operational reserve."

For more information on the history of reserve activations, see CRS Report RL30637, *Involuntary Reserve Activations For U.S. Military Operations Since World War II*, by Lawrence Kapp.

7. How Does the Posse Comitatus Act Affect Use of the Reserve Components to Handle Domestic Problems?

The Posse Comitatus Act (18 U.S.C. 1385), along with other related laws and administrative provisions, prohibits the use of the military to execute civilian laws unless expressly authorized by the Constitution or an act of Congress. As a part of the military, the reserve components are generally covered under these provisions and thus are restricted in the same way that active component forces are. However, there are important exceptions to this general rule.

First, Congress has made a number of exceptions to the Posse Comitatus Act which permit military involvement in law enforcement. For example, Congress has enacted several statutes

---

(...continued)

12304b. DOD was not able to provide a breakout of how many involuntary activations for Kosovo have occurred since 2003.

[35] For figures through FY11, see Office of the Assistant Secretary of Defense, Reserve Affairs, *Command Brief*, slide 15, http://ra.defense.gov/documents/publications/OSDRACommandBrief.pptx. The FY12 figure was provided directly by the Office of the Assistant Secretary of Defense, Reserve Affairs.

which authorize the President to use military forces to suppress insurrections and domestic violence.[36] If these statutes were to be invoked, the President could use the reserve components in the same way as active component forces to put down a rebellion or to control domestic violence. Another important exception relates to the Coast Guard, which Congress has vested with broad law enforcement authority.[37] Under these statutory provisions, the Coast Guard Reserve can participate, like its active counterpart, in the enforcement of maritime, customs, and certain other federal laws.

Second, when acting in its capacity as the organized militia of a state, the National Guard is not part of the federal military and thus is *not* covered by the Posse Comitatus Act. Only when it is called into federal service does the National Guard become subject to the act. As such, the National Guard can be used by state authorities to enforce the law. For example, while acting in a state capacity, the National Guard has been used for riot control and counter-drug activities. More recently, it was used to provide increased security at airports throughout the country in the aftermath of the September 11 terrorist attacks and to assist with security and disaster relief missions in the aftermath of Hurricanes Katrina and Rita.

For more information on the Posse Comitatus Act see CRS Report R42669, *The Posse Comitatus Act and Related Matters: A Sketch*, by Jennifer K. Elsea.

8. What Type of Pay and Benefits Do Reservists Receive for Reserve Duty?

This section focuses on the pay and benefits provided to participating members of the Selected Reserve when they are *not* serving on active duty. In general, when reservists are ordered to federal active duty for more than 30 days they receive pay and benefits virtually identical to those of active duty personnel, although there are some exceptions.[38] When ordered to active duty for a period of 30 days or less, they receive most, but not all, of the pay and benefits that active duty personnel receive.[39] Additionally, reservists who are not on active duty receive a different set of pay and benefits when they are serving in a reserve component category other than the Selected Reserve,[40] and members of the National Guard receive a different set of pay and benefits when they are serving full-time in a state status.[41]

---

[36] See 10 U.S.C. §331-335.

[37] See 14 U.S.C. §2 and §89.

[38] For example, one area in which benefits are not identical is reenlistment bonuses. Reservists serving on active duty who are eligible for a reenlistment bonus may receive a maximum bonus of $15,000 per year of obligated service (37 U.S.C. 331(c)(1)(C)), as opposed to a maximum bonus of $30,000 per year of obligated service for active duty personnel (37 U.S.C. 331(c)(1)(B)). However, reserve bonuses are provided in exchange for continued reserve service, while active duty bonuses are provided in exchange for continued active duty service.

[39] For example, they do not receive medical coverage for their families unless they have enrolled in the new premium-based TRICARE insurance program (see question 13). Additionally, those serving 30 days or less typically receive a housing allowance known as BAH-II, which is generally lower than the normal Basic Allowance for Housing (BAH); however, these individuals receive the normal BAH if they are serving in support of a contingency operation (see 37 U.S.C. 403(g)).

[40] Members of the Selected Reserve receive the most generous package of pay and benefits, although Retired Reservists—whose retirement pay and benefits are deferred compensation for at least twenty years of active and/or reserve service—may receive superior benefits in some respects. Members of the Individual Ready Reserve and the (continued...)

Pay

Members of the Selected Reserve are generally required to work one weekend a month (called inactive duty for training or IDT; also known colloquially as "weekend drill") and two weeks per year (called annual training or AT; also known colloquially as "summer camp"). They are paid for this work according to the same basic pay table used for their active duty counterparts. This table is based on both rank and years of service. Thus, reservists and active duty personnel of the same rank and the same longevity fall into the same category for basic pay. However, reservists and active duty personnel do not always accrue credit for a day of pay in the same manner.

During AT, reservists receive one day of basic pay for each day of duty, just as active duty personnel receive one day of basic pay for each day of duty. Thus, for a typical two week long AT, a reservist receives 14 days of pay. However, during IDT reservists receive one day of pay for each unit training assembly (UTA) they attend. A UTA is generally a four-hour period of instruction, and there are usually four UTAs per drill weekend. Thus, for each two-day long drill weekend reservists receive the equivalent of four days of basic pay. During a typical year then, a reservist who worked 38 days (14 days of annual training plus 24 days of IDT) would receive the equivalent of 62 days' worth of basic pay (14 days of pay for annual training and 48 days of pay for IDT).

Special and Incentive Pays

Depending on the type of duty they are performing, reservists may also be eligible for special and incentive pays for performing certain types of hazardous or arduous duty, for serving in certain assignments, or for possessing certain skills. Reservists are generally eligible for special and incentive pays during AT under the same conditions as active component personnel. Typically, they may receive a pro-rated portion of the full monthly amount corresponding to the number of days served. Reservists may also be eligible for special and incentive pays during IDT, and typically receive such compensation at a rate proportional to the amount of inactive duty compensation they receive (i.e., one-thirtieth of the monthly rate for each unit training assembly).

Allowances

During AT, but not during IDT, reservists may be eligible for a housing allowance known as Basic Allowance for Housing II (BAH-II), which is generally lower than the normal Basic Allowance for Housing (BAH), and for a subsistence allowance known as Basic Allowance for Subsistence (BAS). Reserve officers are also entitled to a $400 clothing allowance at the beginning of their reserve service to assist them in purchasing necessary uniform items. Furthermore, if they are called to active duty for more than 90 days, they are usually entitled to an additional $200 clothing allowance. Reserve enlisted personnel are typically issued all of their uniforms, shoes, boots, and insignia and therefore do not receive any clothing allowance; however, they may be eligible for a clothing allowance if required uniform items are not provided to them.[42]

(...continued)

Standby Reserve are generally not paid and are eligible for only a few benefits.

[41] See questions 10-12.

[42] For clothing allowances, see Department of Defense Financial Management Regulation, Volume 7A, Chapters 29 (continued...)

Medical Care

Until recently, non-activated reservists had only limited access to TRICARE, the military health care system. Specifically, they were entitled to treatment at a military medical facility for illnesses or injuries incurred or aggravated during IDT or AT, while traveling directly to or from their IDT or AT duty station, or while remaining overnight between successive periods of inactive duty training.[43] Family members of reservists have generally not been eligible for military medical care during either IDT or AT, but became eligible if the reservist was ordered to active duty for more than 30 days. All of these provisions are still in effect today, but the 108th and 109th Congress passed several provisions which provide premium-based access to TRICARE for non-activated reservists and their families. These provisions are discussed in more detail later in this report (see "13. Has Congress Made Any Recent Changes in Pay and Benefits for Reserve Component Personnel?").

Dental Care

Members of the Selected Reserve and Individual Ready Reserve are eligible to enroll in a dental plan known as the TRICARE Dental Program (TDP), provided they have at least 12 months of service remaining. The annual premium for the program is about $132 for a member of the Selected Reserve, and about $329 for members of the Individual Ready Reserve. In return, TDP provides up to $1,300 of coverage per year, per beneficiary, towards basic dental care procedures including diagnostic, preventive, and some restorative services, as well as some oral surgery and emergency services. There is also a benefit for orthodontic services, which has a lifetime cap of $1,750 per beneficiary. Members of the Selected Reserve and Individual Ready Reserve may also enroll their family in the TDP, but doing so increases the annual premium by about $987 per year.

Life Insurance

Members of the Selected Reserve are eligible to purchase up to $400,000 of life insurance under the Servicemembers' Group Life Insurance (SGLI) program. The major benefits of this program are its relatively low cost and its guarantee of payment even if death occurs as a result of combat action (something private insurers do not always provide). Reservists who participate in SGLI can also purchase up to $100,000 of life insurance for their spouses and are provided with $10,000 of life insurance coverage per child at no cost.

Commissary and Exchange Privileges

Members of the Selected Reserve and their family members have unlimited access to the commissary, a system of subsidized military supermarkets.[44] Members of the Selected Reserve

---

(...continued)

and 30, http://comptroller.defense.gov/Portals/45/documents/fmr/current/07a/Volume_07a.pdf.

[43] 10 U.S.C. 1074a.

[44] Unlimited access to the commissary for members of the Selected Reserve and their family members was included in the FY2004 National Defense Authorization Act (P.L. 108-136, Section 651). Prior to that, members of the Selected Reserve and their family members were limited to 24 visits per year.

and their family members also have unlimited access to the military exchange system, a system of military department stores.

Retirement

Reservists become eligible for retirement after 20 years of qualifying service.[45] A year of qualifying service is defined as a year in which a reservist has earned at least 50 "retirement points." Reservists earn 15 retirement points per year simply for being a member of the Ready Reserve, one point for each unit training assembly (UTA), one point for each day of annual training (AT), and one point for each day of active duty. Points can also be earned for completing certain military correspondence or distance learning courses and for performing funeral honors duty. Earning 50 points in a given year is usually not difficult for members of the Selected Reserve, as attending all weekend drills and two weeks of annual training will generate 77 retirement points.[46] Point totals are also important because they are used to calculate retired pay (see below). Excluding points earned while in an active duty status (which includes annual training), reservists may not earn more than 130 points per year.[47] Additionally, including points earned while in an active duty status, reservists may not earn more than 365 points in a year (366 in a leap year).

After completing 20 years of qualifying service, a reservist may apply for retirement. Upon retirement, *but before reaching the retired pay eligibility age*, a reservist is entitled to a limited number of benefits, including unlimited use of the military exchange, commissary system, and other military facilities, and space available travel on military aircraft within the United States and its territories. Upon reaching the retired pay eligibility age—which can range between 50 and 60 depending on how many days of certain types of duty the reservist performed during his career[48]—the retired reservist is eligible to receive retired pay. At age 60, the retired reservist is entitled to benefits identical to those of active duty retirees, including space-available travel on military aircraft throughout the world and access to military health care benefits.

Retired pay is calculated by totaling all the points earned during all the years of service and then dividing this sum by 360. This calculation produces the number of "equivalent years" of active duty service the reservist has performed. The number of "equivalent years" is then multiplied by 2.5% to determine the "retirement benefit multiplier." This multiplier is then applied to an amount based on the monthly base pay earned by an active duty service member with similar rank and years of service.[49]

---

[45] One can also earn credit towards reserve retirement while serving in the Individual Ready Reserve.

[46] Fifteen points for "reserve membership," 48 points for attending 48 unit training assemblies during weekend drill, and 14 points for attending a two-week long Annual Training.

[47] The annual point "cap" has changed over time. Excluding points earned while in an active duty status, a reservist could not earn more than: 60 in any one year of service before the year of service that includes September 23, 1996; 75 in the year of service that includes September 23, 1996, and in any subsequent year of service before the year of service that includes October 30, 2000; 90 in the year of service that includes October 30, 2000, and in any subsequent year of service before the year of service that includes October 30, 2007; and 130 in the year of service that includes October 30, 2007, and subsequent years. See 10 U.S.C. 12733. The increase to 130 points per year was included in Section 648 of the National Defense Authorization Act for FY2008.

[48] This is a comparatively recent change in the law, based on Section 647 of the National Defense Authorization Act for FY2008. Previously, reservists became eligible for retired pay at age 60. See Question 13 for more information.

[49] For reservists who entered the military before September 8, 1980, the amount is the same as the base pay rate of an active duty service member with the same rank and years of service. For reservists who entered military service on or (continued...)

For example, a reservist who accrues 2,500 points over the course of 20 qualifying years would be deemed to have completed the equivalent of 6.94 years of active service (2,500 divided by 360). This figure, when multiplied by 2.5%, produces a multiplier of 17.3%. Assuming that the basic pay for an active duty service-member with similar rank and longevity was $3,000 per month, the reservist would be entitled to retired pay in the amount of $519 per month (17.3% of $3,000).

9. How Are Reservists Called to Active Duty by the Federal Government? How Often Does this Happen? After Activation, How Long Can They Be Required to Serve on Active Duty?

At present, there are four major statutory provisions by which reservists can be involuntarily ordered to active duty by the federal government for an extended period of time, and another provision for involuntarily activating members of the federal reserve components for short periods of time to respond to disasters or emergencies.[50] (For a discussion of additional ways in which members of the National Guard can be called up in a nonfederal status, see "11. Are There Other Ways in Which Members of the National Guard Can Be Activated?") These provisions differ from each other in terms of the statutory requirements for utilization, the number and category of reservists called up, and the duration of the call up. Three of these authorities have been in existence for decades, and are commonly referred to as Full Mobilization, Partial Mobilization, and Presidential Reserve Call-up (PRC). The other two authorities, added in 2011, do not yet have common names, but are referred to in this report as Combatant Command Support Activation and Disaster Response Activation. There is also a special provision for the recall of retired reservists. Each of these authorities is detailed below.

Full Mobilization

In time of war or national emergency declared by Congress, or when otherwise authorized by law, Section 12301(a) of Title 10 U.S.C. permits the Service Secretaries[51] to authorize the involuntary

---

(...continued)

after that date, the amount is the average of the highest 36 months of basic pay he or she would have been entitled to on active duty.

[50] There is also a statutory provision, 10 U.S.C. 12301(b), which allows the Secretary of a military department to involuntarily order reservists to active duty "for not more than 15 days per year."

[51] Section 12301(a) of Title 10 U.S.C. states "In time of war or of national emergency declared by the Congress, or when otherwise authorized by law, an authority designated by the Secretary concerned may, without the consent of the persons affected, order any unit, and any member not assigned to a unit organized to serve as a unit, of a reserve component under the jurisdiction of that Secretary to active duty for the duration of the war or emergency and for six months thereafter. However a member on an inactive status list or in a retired status may not be ordered to active duty under this subsection unless the Secretary concerned, with the approval of the Secretary of Defense in the case of a Secretary of a military department, determines that there are not enough qualified Reserves in an active status or in the inactive National Guard in the required category who are readily available." The "Secretary concerned," as defined in 10 U.S.C. 101(a)(9), is the Secretary of the Army with respect to the Army, the Secretary of the Air Force with respect to the Air Force, the Secretary of the Navy with respect to the Navy, Marine Corps, and Coast Guard (when it is (continued...)

---

activation of any member of the reserve components under his or her jurisdiction. There is no limit on the number of reservists which may be ordered to active duty under this provision and mobilized reservists may be kept on active duty for the duration of the war or emergency plus six months.

Partial Mobilization

In time of a national emergency declared by the President, or when otherwise authorized by law, Section 12302 of Title 10 U.S.C. permits the Service Secretaries[52] to authorize the involuntary activation of members of the Ready Reserve under his or her jurisdiction for a period not to exceed 24 consecutive months. Up to 1 million members of the Ready Reserve may serve on active duty at any one time under this provision of law. Reservists may be mobilized under this provision of law without approval from Congress. This authority was used to mobilize reservists during the later part of the Persian Gulf War (1991) when the PRC authority was no longer sufficient to activate the number of reservists needed. President George W. Bush invoked this authority in the aftermath of the September 11th terrorist attacks. It was used to mobilize reservists for Operations Noble Eagle and Enduring Freedom, and later used for Operation Iraqi Freedom/New Dawn as well.[53] Activations under this authority have continued to the present.

(...continued)

operating as part of the Department of the Navy), and the Secretary of Homeland Security with respect to the Coast Guard (when it is not operating as part of the Department of the Navy). Although the law assigns authority to mobilize reservists to an official designated by "the Secretary concerned," the President is ultimately responsible for the decision to order reservists to active duty.

[52] Section 12302 of Title 10 U.S.C. states "In time of national emergency declared by the President after January 1, 1953, or when otherwise authorized by law, an authority designated by the Secretary concerned may, without the consent of the persons concerned, order any unit, and any member not assigned to a unit organized to serve as a unit, in the Ready Reserve under the jurisdiction of that Secretary to active duty for not more than 24 consecutive months." See footnote 51 for the definition of "Secretary concerned." While the law assigns authority to mobilize reservists to an official designated by "the Secretary concerned," the President is ultimately responsible for the decision to order reservists to active duty.

[53] Until 2007, DOD's general policy had been to mobilize reservists for no more than one year, while allowing the Service Secretaries to keep reservists on active duty for up to 24 *cumulative* months if they were needed to meet operational or other requirements. No reservist was allowed to serve beyond 24 cumulative months under the Partial Mobilization authority. Army Reserve and National Guard units deploying to Iraq and Afghanistan were typically mobilized for 18 months to provide for pre-deployment training, a one-year tour in theater, demobilization, and the utilization of accrued leave prior to release from active duty. On January 19, 2007, Secretary of Defense Robert Gates established a new policy with respect to the exercise of Partial Mobilization in support of these operations. The new policy specified that "from this point forward, involuntary mobilization for members of the Reserve Forces shall be for a maximum of one year at a time. At service discretion, this period may exclude individual skill training required for deployment and post-mobilization leave ... the planning objective for involuntary mobilization of Guard/Reserve units will remain a one year mobilized to five year demobilized ratio. However, today's global demands will require a number of selected Guard/Reserve units to be remobilized sooner than this standard." In practice, this new policy limits reserve mobilizations to about 13 or 14 months at a time for the vast majority of reservists (the exception would be those reservist who need lengthy individual skill training to become qualified in their occupational specialty prior to deployment). Note, however, there is no longer a prohibition on serving more than 24 *cumulative* months under the Partial Mobilization authority. This is consistent with the statutory language of 10 U.S.C. 12302, which only specifies a 24 *consecutive* month cap.

Presidential Reserve Call-up (PRC)

Section 12304 of Title 10 U.S.C. permits the President to authorize the involuntarily activation of members of the Selected Reserve and the Individual Ready Reserve for a period up to 365 consecutive days.[54] Under this authority, up to 200,000 members of the Selected Reserve and the Individual Ready Reserve "mobilization category"—a sub-component of the Individual Ready Reserve which is currently not being used[55]—may serve on active duty at one time. The President may activate reservists under this provision of law without approval from Congress; however, he is required to notify Congress within 24 hours of such an action. This authority was used to mobilize reservists during the earlier part of the Persian Gulf War (1990-1991), during the intervention in Haiti (1994-1996), during the Bosnian peacekeeping mission (1995-2004), during the low-intensity conflict with Iraq[56] (1998-2003), and during the earlier years of the Kosovo conflict and peacekeeping mission (1999-present).[57] Those activated under this authority may not be used to enforce federal authority or to suppress insurrection; nor may they be used to provide assistance to the federal government or the states for disaster response, unless responding to an emergency involving the use or threatened use of weapons of mass destruction or an actual or threatened terrorist attack of significant proportions.[58]

Combatant Command Support Activation

The National Defense Authorization Act for Fiscal Year 2012 contained a provision to allow involuntarily activations of Selected Reserve units for up to 365 consecutive days of active duty.[59] No more than 60,000 members of the National Guard and Reserves may be serving on active duty under this authority at any given time. The authority to activate reservists under this provision rests with the Service Secretary, but it may only be invoked for a "preplanned mission in support of a combatant command" where the costs of the activations and a description of the mission are included in the service's budget materials. According to the committee report which accompanied the Senate version of the bill, this new authority "is not designed for use for emergent operational or humanitarian missions, but rather to enhance the use of reserve component units that organize, train, and plan to support operational mission requirements to the same standards as active component units under service force generation plans in a cyclic, periodic, and predictable

---

[54] Section 522, P.L. 109-364, the John Warner National Defense Authorization Act for FY2007, expanded this call-up period from 270 to 365 days.

[55] The law specifies that the only members of the Individual Ready Reserve who may be activated under a PRC are those individuals who belong to "the Individual Ready Reserve mobilization category and designated as essential under regulations prescribed by the Secretary concerned." Further, 10 U.S.C. 10144(b) specifies that individuals may not be placed in this mobilization category unless "(A) the member volunteers for that category; and (B) the member is selected for that category by the Secretary concerned, based upon the needs of the service and the grade and military skills of that member." DOD has not made it a priority to fill this "mobilization category" and currently there are no members assigned to it. Thus, the PRC authority is effectively limited to members of the Selected Reserve at present. If this mobilization category were to be manned and used, the law limits the total number of IRR "mobilization category" members on active duty at one time to 30,000.

[56] See footnote 30.

[57] See footnote 34

[58] 10 U.S.C. 12304(b) and (c). The authority to use those activated under a PRC for domestic response missions was expanded by Section 1076(c) of the John Warner National Defense Authorization Act for FY2007 (P.L. 109-364); however, this provision was repealed by Section 1068(c) of the National Defense Authorization Act for FY2008 (P.L. 110-181).

[59] P.L. 112-81, Section 516.

---

manner."[60] This provision is now codified at 10 U.S.C. 12304b. In its FY2014 and FY2015 budget requests, the Army specified its plans to use this authority for an array of smaller on-going operations.[61]

Disaster Response Activation

A separate provision in the National Defense Authorization Act for Fiscal Year 2012, now codified at 10 U.S.C. 12304a, allows the Secretary of Defense to involuntarily order units and individuals of the Army Reserve, Navy Reserve, Marine Corps Reserve, and Air Force Reserve to active duty for up to 120 days "when a governor requests federal assistance in responding to a major disaster or emergency."[62] National Guard forces are not included in this authority, but state governors already have the ability to activate their state National Guard forces and to request support from other state National Guards under the Emergency Management Assistance Compact. The Coast Guard Reserve already has a short-term, disaster response activation authority (14 U.S.C. 712).

This provision also contained language specifying that when the Armed Forces and the National Guard are employed simultaneously in support of civil authorities within the United States, a dual status commander should be appointed. A dual status commander is a military officer who simultaneously serves as a state National Guard officer under the control of his or her governor, and as a federal military officer under the control of the President.[63] A dual status commander is thus able to command nonfederalized National Guard forces and federal forces via these separate chains of command. The language of this provision also specifies that "when a major disaster or emergency occurs in any area subject to the laws of any State, Territory, or the District of Columbia, the Governor of the State affected normally should be the principal authority supported by the primary Federal agency and its supporting Federal entities, and the Adjutant General of the State or his or her subordinate designee normally should be the principal military authority supported by the dual-status commander when acting in his or her State capacity."[64]

Recall of Retired Reservists

Members of the Retired Reserve can be involuntarily ordered to active duty in the case of a Full Mobilization (see "Full Mobilization," above). Under this authority, there is no limit on the number of retired reservists who can be called to active duty, and they may be kept on active duty for the duration of the war or emergency plus six months. Additionally, the Secretary of each military department has the authority to involuntarily order certain members of the Retired Reserve to active duty at any time, but this authority only applies to members of the Retired

---

[60] S.Rept. 112-26, p. 110.

[61] For FY2014, see pages 9-10 of the Army's Military Personnel budget justification book, available here: http://asafm.army mil/Documents/OfficeDocuments/Budget/budgetmaterials/fy14/milpers//mpa.pdf . For FY2015, see pages 11-12 of this the Army's Military Personnel budget justification book, available here: http://asafm.army mil/ Documents/OfficeDocuments/Budget/budgetmaterials/fy15/milpers//mpa.pdf

[62] P.L. 112-81, Section 515. The language does not limit the activations only to the Selected Reserve, so it appears that members of the Individual Ready Reserve can be activated under this authority.

[63] See 32 U.S.C. 315 and 325.

[64] P.L. 112-81, Section 515(c).

Reserve who have a regular retirement (at least 20 years of active duty).[65] There is a limit on the amount of time recalled retirees can serve, and a limit on the number of officers recalled, but these limits do not apply in times of war or national emergency declared by the Congress or the President.[66]

10. What Type of Pay, Benefits, and Legal Protections Are Provided to Reservists Mobilized for Operations Noble Eagle and Enduring Freedom?

All reservists serving in Operations Enduring Freedom are serving in a federal status in support of a contingency operation.[67] As such, they are entitled to pay, benefits, and legal protections which are virtually identical to those provided to active duty servicemembers. Specifically, they are entitled to basic pay at the same rate as active duty and, if qualified, may receive special and incentive pays including Hazardous Duty Pay, Aviation Career Incentive Pay, Hostile Fire/Imminent Danger Pay, and special pays for health professionals. They are also entitled to a variety of allowances that are not taxable, including Basic Allowance for Housing (BAH), Basic Allowance for Subsistence (BAS), and, if separated from their families, a Family Separation Allowance (FSA). Medical and dental coverage for these reservists and their family members is virtually identical to that provided to active duty servicemembers, provided the orders are for more than 30 days.[68] Leave is accrued in the same manner as for active duty personnel. They are also allowed to use legal assistance, child care centers, space available travel, and morale, welfare and recreation (MWR) services.[69] Finally, they are protected by both the Uniformed Services Employment and Reemployment Rights Act (USERRA) and the Servicemembers' Civil Relief Act (SCRA).[70]

The status of reservists serving in support of Operation Noble Eagle is more varied. Some have been called up in a strictly federal status and are, therefore, receiving pay, benefits, and legal protections identical to those of reservists serving in support of Operation Enduring Freedom. Certain members of the National Guard have been called up in a purely state status, or under state control but with federal pay and benefits. They receive a different set of pay, benefits, and protections. For more information on these distinctions, see "11. Are There Other Ways in Which Members of the National Guard Can Be Activated?" and "12. What Type of Legal Protections Do

---

[65] 10 U.S.C. 688(b)(2).

[66] 10 U.S.C. 688 & 690.

[67] As were all reservists who served in Operations Enduring Freedom or Iraqi Freedom/New Dawn in the past.

[68] Those servicemembers with orders for 30 days or less would be eligible for any illness or injury incurred in the line of duty. However, their families would not be eligible for TRICARE benefits unless they were enrolled in the new TRICARE Reserve Select program (see "13. Has Congress Made Any Recent Changes in Pay and Benefits for Reserve Component Personnel?").

[69] However, as the families of activated reservists often do not live near the military bases where these services are provided, taking advantage of these services may be difficult. Additionally, waiting lists can limit access to child care services.

[70] For more information on USERRA and SCRA, see "12. What Type of Legal Protections Do Reservists Have When They Are Serving on Active Duty? What Reemployment Rights Do Reservists Have after Being Released from Active Duty?"

Reservists Have When They Are Serving on Active Duty? What Reemployment Rights Do Reservists Have after Being Released from Active Duty?"

11. Are There Other Ways in Which Members of the National Guard Can Be Activated?

Yes. Owing to the unique status of the National Guard as both a state and federal organization (see "5. What Is the Difference Between the "Reserves" and the "National Guard"?"), they can be called to active duty either in an exclusively federal status, in an exclusively state status, or under state control with federal pay and benefits.

As members of the Reserve Component, National Guardsmen can be called to *federal* active duty in the same way as other reservists (see "9. How Are Reservists Called to Active Duty by the Federal Government? How Often Does this Happen? After Activation, How Long Can They Be Required to Serve on Active Duty?"). When this happens, control passes from the governor of the affected units and personnel to the President of the United States. When in federal service, Guard units and personnel typically perform military training or participate in military operations and they are entitled to the same pay, benefits, and legal protections as other reservists in federal service.[71]

As members of the militia of their state or territory, National Guard personnel can also be called up by their governor for full-time duty. When employed in this capacity, referred to as state active duty, National Guardsmen are considered state or territorial employees, not federal employees, and their pay and benefits are determined by state or territorial law. They are not eligible for protection under the Servicemembers' Civil Relief Act or the Uniformed Services Employment and Reemployment Rights Act (see "12. What Type of Legal Protections Do Reservists Have When They Are Serving on Active Duty? What Reemployment Rights Do Reservists Have after Being Released from Active Duty?"), although they may be protected by analogous laws enacted at the state level. Typical missions performed under state active duty include responding to disasters and civil disorders. Additionally, shortly after September 11, 2001, some governors called up members of the National Guard to protect critical infrastructure in their states, such as nuclear power plants, water treatment facilities, and bridges, from potential terrorist attacks.

A third form of duty for National Guard personnel involves duty under state control but with pay and benefits provided by the federal government. This is sometimes referred to as "Title 32 status" in reference to the part of the U.S. Code which governs this duty status. Typical duties performed in this status include inactive duty for training (IDT or "weekend drill") and annual training (AT) within the United States. Another type of duty which falls in this category is specified in Title 32 of the U.S. Code, Section 502(f). This provision of law provides that "a member of the National Guard may ... without his consent, but with the pay and allowances provided by law ... be ordered to perform training or other duty in addition to that prescribed under subsection (a) [i.e., IDT or AT]."[72] This is the provision of law which was used to provide

---

[71] When they are ordered to federal active duty for more than 30 days, reservists receive benefits nearly identical to service members on active duty. When ordered to active duty in for a period of 30 days or less, they receive most, but not all, of the benefits which active duty personnel receive. (See questions 8 and 10 for more information on these topics).

[72] 32 U.S.C. §502(f)(1). The training or duty ordered to be performed under this provision of law may include the (continued...)

federal pay and benefits to the Guardsmen called up to provide security at many of the nation's airports in the aftermath of the terrorist attacks of September 11, 2001, to assist with the response to Hurricanes Katrina and Rita in 2005, and for the southwest border security mission in 2006-2008 and 2010-2014. Guardsmen called up under this authority receive federal pay and benefits, and are entitled to certain legal protections[73] as though they were in federal service, but they otherwise operate in a manner similar to state duty.

12. What Type of Legal Protections Do Reservists Have When They Are Serving on Active Duty? What Reemployment Rights Do Reservists Have after Being Released from Active Duty?

When they are called into active federal service, reservists become eligible for a broad array of legal protections. Many of these protections are contained in the Servicemembers' Civil Relief Act (SCRA, P.L. 108-189), which amended and renamed the Soldiers' and Sailors' Civil Relief Act (SSCRA) of 1940.[74] (Note, however, that National Guardsmen who are serving in a state status are not covered by the SCRA. National Guardsmen performing full time National Guard duty under Title 32 of the U.S. Code are covered by the SCRA in certain circumstances.)[75] Among other things, the SCRA provides most people called to active duty with certain protections against rental property evictions, mortgage foreclosures, insurance cancellations, and government property seizures to pay tax bills. It also limits the amount of interest that the activated service member has to pay on loans incurred prior to activation to 6%.[76] For a more

---

(...continued)

following: "(A)Support of operations or missions undertaken by the member's unit at the request of the President or Secretary of Defense. (B) Support of training operations and training missions assigned in whole or in part to the National Guard by the Secretary concerned, but only to the extent that such training missions and training operations— (i) are performed in the United States or the Commonwealth of Puerto Rico or possessions of the United States; and (ii) are only to instruct active duty military, foreign military (under the same authorities and restrictions applicable to active duty troops), Department of Defense contractor personnel, or Department of Defense civilian employees." 32 U.S.C. §502(f)(2).

[73] Specifically, they are entitled to protection under the Uniformed Services Employment and Reemployment Rights Act (USERRA), but are only covered under the Servicemembers' Civil Relief Act (SCRA) if performing "service under a call to active service authorized by the President or the Secretary of Defense for a period of more than 30 consecutive days under Section 502(f) of Title 32, United States Code, for purposes of responding to a national emergency declared by the President and supported by Federal funds" (P.L. 108-189, Section 101(2)(A)(ii), codified at 50 U.S.C. App. 511). Those not covered by the SCRA may, however, receive civil liability protection from state or territorial laws.

[74] 50 U.S.C. App. 501 et. seq.

[75] See footnote 73. See questions 5 and 11 for more information on nonfederal status for National Guardsmen.

[76] Note, however, that the SCRA did not apply to student loans until recently. "Historically, federally guaranteed student loans were not eligible for the 6% interest rate cap. Section 428(d) of the Federal Family Education Loan Program, addressing applicability of usury laws, excluded the SCRA interest rate limitation on those loans. P.L. 110-315, the Higher Education Opportunity Act, amended Section 428(d) to explicitly permit application of the SCRA interest rate cap on federally guaranteed student loans. As of August 14, 2008, federally guaranteed student loans are treated like all other debts incurred prior to entering active duty. Loans disbursed prior to enactment of the amendment are not covered and therefore are not subject to the 6% interest rate limitation. Additionally, servicemembers currently on active duty that received loans prior to entering active duty will not be able to claim the 6% cap." CRS Report (continued...)

---

complete description of the legal protections provided to activated reservists by the SCRA, see CRS Report RL34575, *The Servicemembers Civil Relief Act (SCRA): An Explanation*, by R. Chuck Mason.

Reservists' employment and reemployment rights are covered under the Uniformed Services Employment and Reemployment Rights Act (USERRA) of 1994.[77] USERRA prohibits employers from discriminating against reservists—including National Guard personnel performing full-time National Guard duty under Title 32 of the U.S. Code, but not those performing state active duty (see "11. Are There Other Ways in Which Members of the National Guard Can Be Activated?")— with respect to hiring, retention, promotion, or other benefits and requires employers to give these individuals time off for military service, regardless of whether the service is voluntary or involuntary.[78] This time off is treated as a furlough or leave of absence,[79] and the reservist may not be required to use vacation leave, annual leave, or similar leave.[80] Upon the completion of such military service, USERRA generally gives the reservist a right to reemployment.[81]

Although there are some exceptions, a reservist is usually entitled to be promptly reemployed by his or her civilian employer and, depending on certain factors, to be reinstated to either (1) the job that the person would have held if the reservist's employment had not been interrupted by military service, (2) the job which the reservist actually held at the time military service began, or (3) a job comparable to the one the reservist held at the time military service began. A comparable job is one of similar pay, status, and seniority that the reservist is qualified to perform.

Finally, upon reinstatement, the reservist is entitled not only to the seniority and seniority-based benefits he or she held at the time military service began but also to any additional seniority and seniority-based benefits that the reservist *would have earned* if he or she had remained continuously employed.[82] For example, suppose a reservist has nine years of seniority with his or her civilian employer and then leaves to perform two years of military service. Upon returning to work at the end of that two-year period, the reservist will be considered to have 11 years of seniority with the civilian employer, and all the rights and benefits that go with that. USERRA also provides certain protection to reservists with respect to job retraining, employer provided health care plans, and employer provided pension plans.[83]

Reservists do have an obligation to notify their employer as soon as possible about upcoming military service. They also have an obligation to report to work, or to notify their employers that

---

(...continued)

RL34575, *The Servicemembers Civil Relief Act (SCRA): An Explanation*, by R. Chuck Mason, p. 11.

[77] 38 U.S.C. Chapter 43. USERRA protects not only reservists, but also those who choose to serve in the active component military for less than five years.

[78] 38 U.S.C. 4311(a).

[79] 38 U.S.C. 4316 (b)(A).

[80] 38 U.S.C. 4316(d). Reservists may, however, choose to use their vacation leave, annual leave, or similar leave while they are performing military service. Some reservists choose to do this so that they can continue to receive pay from their civilian employer while away on military duty.

[81] 38 U.S.C. 4312.

[82] 38 U.S.C. 4316.

[83] 38 U.S.C. 4313, 4317, 4318.

they intend to report to work, within a relatively short time after being released from active duty. Failure to meet these obligations may effectively nullify a reservist's right to reemployment.[84]

Reservists who believe their civilian employer has violated their rights under USERRA have several options. The first is to contact their commanding officer, who may be able to resolve the issue with the employer. Alternatively, reservists may contact the National Committee for Employer Support of the Guard and Reserve (NCESGR), a Department of Defense organization which will contact the employer and attempt to resolve the problem informally. A complaint can also be made to the Veterans' Employment and Training Service (VETS) of the Department of Labor. VETS has the power to investigate complaints and attempt to resolve them through mediation. If that fails, the servicemember may request that VETS refer the case to the Office of Special Counsel (for federal employees) or the Department of Justice (for those who are not federal employees). "If the Attorney General is reasonably satisfied that the Service Member is entitled to relief, the Attorney General may exercise DOJ's prosecutorial authority and commence an action in Federal court on behalf of the Service Member."[85] The Office of Special Counsel reviews cases of federal employees in a similar manner and may represent the servicemember before the Merit Systems Protection Board (MSPB).[86] Additionally, servicemembers have the option of hiring a private attorney to pursue a claim in court or before the MSPB.[87]

13. Has Congress Made Any Recent Changes in Pay and Benefits for Reserve Component Personnel?

Yes. In recent years Congress has made a number of significant changes in Reserve Component pay and benefits. The most significant of those changes are (1) establishing a premium-based TRICARE benefit for non-activated reservists, (2) creating new educational benefits for reservists who have been mobilized since September 11, 2001, (3) providing additional compensation for certain reservists who experience a reduction in income when activated, and (4) lowering the age at which certain reservists can draw retired pay below 60. Each of these changes is discussed below.

Premium-based Access to TRICARE for Non-Activated Reservists and their Families

When ordered to federal active duty for more than 30 days, members of the National Guard and Reserves are entitled to receive medical benefits under TRICARE (the military's health care

---

[84] 38 U.S.C. 4312 (e).

[85] Department of Labor, Office of the Assistant Secretary for Veterans' Employment and Training, *Uniformed Services Employment and Reemployment Rights Act of 1994 (USERRA), Fiscal Year 2011 Annual Report to Congress*, July 2012, p. 5, http://www.dol.gov/vets/programs/userra/2011USERRAReport.pdf. This report contains a useful summary of USERRA enforcement processes on pages 4-7.

[86] A somewhat different process is followed for federal employees of the following agencies: "the Federal Bureau of Investigation, the Central Intelligence Agency, the Defense Intelligence Agency, the National Geospatial-Intelligence Agency, the National Security Agency, and, as determined by the President, any Executive agency or unit thereof the principal function of which is the conduct of foreign intelligence or counterintelligence activities" (5 U.S.C. §2302(a)(2)(C)(ii)) See 38 U.S.C. §4325.

[87] See 38 U.S.C. 4323(a)(3) and 4324(b).

---

system) for themselves and their family members. However, until recently, non-activated reservists had limited access to TRICARE for themselves and no access for their families. This began to change in 108th and 109th Congresses, both of which passed provisions expanding access to TRICARE for non-activated reservists and their families.

In 2004, Congress authorized the TRICARE Reserve Select (TRS) program for Reserve Component members.[88] The program has gone through several modifications since then, but it currently permits most members of the Selected Reserve who are not on active duty to obtain coverage similar to that of TRICARE Standard and TRICARE Extra by paying a premium of 28% of the total costs of their coverage.[89] The premiums for TRS coverage through December 2014 are $51.68 per month for an individual reservist, and $204.29 per month for the reservist and his family members.[90]

New Educational Benefit for Activated Reservists

Both the 108th and 110th Congresses passed legislation which provides enhanced "GI Bill" type educational benefits for reservists who have served in support of a contingency operation since September 11, 2001. Prior to passage of these laws, there were two main educational assistance programs for currently serving military personnel: the Montgomery G.I. Bill-Active Duty[91] (MGIB-AD) and the Montgomery G.I. Bill-Selected Reserve[92] (MGIB-SR).[93]

Eligibility for the basic MGIB-AD benefit typically requires three years of continuous active duty service and a deduction totaling $1,200 from the servicemembers' pay.[94] The basic benefit for

---

[88] Ronald W. Reagan National Defense Authorization Act for FY2005, P.L. 108-375, Section 701.

[89] The 108th Congress passed legislation allowing certain members of the Selected Reserve and their family members to receive coverage under the TRICARE Standard option. To be eligible, the reservist must have served on active duty in support of a contingency operation since September 11, 2001, and had to sign an agreement to continue serving in the Selected Reserve. The duration of eligibility was set at a maximum of one year for each 90 days of service, or for the duration of the service agreement, whichever was shorter. Additionally, the reservist would have to pay a premium, set at 28% of the amount which the Secretary of Defense determined to be actuarially reasonable. The 109th Congress established two new "tiers" to the TRS program. The first new tier provided coverage under the TRICARE Standard option to members of the Selected Reserve who committed to one year of continued service in the Selected Reserve and who were either (a) "eligible unemployment compensation recipients,"(b) ineligible for health care benefits under an employer sponsored health benefits plan, or (c) self-employed. These reservists would have had to pay a premium set at 50% of the amount which the Secretary of Defense determined to be actuarially reasonable. The second new tier provided coverage under the TRICARE Standard option to those members of the Selected Reserve who do not qualify under the original TRS or the unemployed/uninsured tier mentioned above, and who committed to one year of continued service in the Selected Reserve. These reservists would have had to pay a premium set at 85% of the amount which the Secretary of Defense determined to be actuarially reasonable. Before the new tiered system could be implemented, Congress passed the FY2007 John Warner National Defense Authorization Act (P.L. 109-364) which replaced the three-tiered program with a single program that permits non-activated reservists to obtain TRICARE coverage by paying a premium of 28% of the total costs of their coverage. Members of the Selected Reserve who are eligible for the Federal Employees Health Benefits Program are not eligible for TRS.

[90] TRICARE Reserve Select (TRS), http://www.tricare mil/Costs/HealthPlanCosts/TRS.aspx .

[91] Title 38, Chapter 30, United States Code.

[92] Title 10, Chapter 1606, United States Code.

[93] For more information on these programs, see CRS Report R42785, *GI Bills Enacted Prior to 2008 and Related Veterans' Educational Assistance Programs: A Primer*, by Cassandria Dortch.

[94] Certain individuals with remaining entitlement under prior GI Bills were also eligible to transfer to the MGIB-AD. A reduced benefit amount of up to $1,339 per month—as of October 1, 2013—is also available for certain individuals who serve at least two years of active duty if the initial obligated period of active duty was less than three years; they (continued...)

---

full-time study provided by MGIB-AD is $1,648 per month, as of October 1, 2013, for up to 36 months. Eligibility for the MGIB-SR benefit requires a six-year commitment to serve in the Selected Reserve, but requires no contributions on the part of the reservist. The educational benefit for full-time study provided by this program is $362 per month, as of October 1, 2013, for up to 36 months. Although the MGIB-SR program requires no contribution (as the MGIB-AD program does), the monthly payments under MGIB-SR are about 22% of the amount of those made under MGIB-AD. While reservists who served on active duty for at least 24 consecutive months were eligible for a reduced MGIB-AD benefit (provided they contributed $1,200 like their active duty peers), those reservists who served less than 24 consecutive months generally remained eligible only for the MGIB-SR until 2004 when Congress established the Reserve Educational Assistance Program.

Reserve Educational Assistance Program

In 2004, Congress established a new program to provide enhanced educational benefits to reservists who were "called or ordered to active service in response to a war or national emergency declared by the President or the Congress, in recognition of the sacrifices that those members make in answering the call to duty."[95] Under this new program, called the Reserve Educational Assistance Program (REAP) by the Department of Veterans' Affairs, eligible reservists[96] receive the following educational benefit for full time study for up to 36 months: 40% of the MGIB-AD basic benefit for those serving at least 90 consecutive days but less than one consecutive year; 60% of the MGIB-AD basic benefit for those serving at least one consecutive year but less than two consecutive years; and 80% of the MGIB-AD basic benefit for those serving at least two consecutive years or three aggregate years.[97] As of October 1, 2013, the 40% benefit equates to $659.20 per month, the 60% benefit equates to $988.80 per month, and the 80% benefit equates to $1,318.40 per month. REAP does not require any contribution on the part

---

(...continued)

are also required to contribute $1,200 to become eligible for the program.

[95] P.L. 108-375, Ronald W. Reagan National Defense Authorization Act for FY2005, Section 527, October 28, 2004. Codified at Chapter 1607 of Title 10.

[96] The eligibility requirements specified in the statute (10 U.S.C. 16163) are as follows:

"(a) ELIGIBILITY—On or after September 11, 2001, a member of a reserve component is entitled to educational assistance under this chapter if the member—(1) served on active duty in support of a contingency operation for 90 consecutive days or more; or (2) in the case of a member of the Army National Guard of the United States or Air National Guard of the United States, performed full time National Guard duty under Section 502(f) of Title 32 for 90 consecutive days or more when authorized by the President or Secretary of Defense for the purpose of responding to a national emergency declared by the President and supported by Federal funds.

(b) DISABLED MEMBERS.—Notwithstanding the eligibility requirements in subsection (a), a member who was ordered to active service as prescribed under subsection (a)(1) or (a)(2) but is released from duty before completing 90 consecutive days because of an injury, illness or disease incurred or aggravated in the line of duty shall be entitled to educational assistance under this chapter at the rate prescribed in Section 16162(c)(4)(A) of this title." [This refers to the 40% rate].

"Contingency operation" is defined in Section 101(a)(13)(B) of Title 10, and includes military operations which "results in the call or order to, or retention on, active duty of members of the uniformed services under section 688, 12301(a), 12302, 12304, 12304a, 12305, or 12406 of this title, chapter 15 of this title, section 712 of title 14, or any other provision of law during a war or during a national emergency declared by the President or Congress." One of the new activation authorities (12304a, Disaster Response Activation) is included in this definition, while the other (12304b, Combatant Command Support Activation) is not.

[97] For more information on this program, see CRS Report R42785, *GI Bills Enacted Prior to 2008 and Related Veterans' Educational Assistance Programs: A Primer*, by Cassandria Dortch.

---

of reservists like the MGIB-AD program does. Originally, eligibility continued only so long as the individual remained in the Selected Reserve (for those activated while serving in the Selected Reserve) or the Individual Ready Reserve/Inactive National Guard (for those activated while serving in the Individual Ready Reserve/Inactive National Guard). However, the 110th Congress amended the REAP law, retroactive to the original provision's date of enactment, allowing members of the Selected Reserve entitled to this benefit to use it for up to 10 years after separating from the Selected Reserve.[98]

Post-9/11 Veterans Educational Assistance Act

The Post-9/11 Veterans Educational Assistance Act of 2008, also known as the Post-9/11 GI Bill, is a new educational benefit passed by the 110th Congress. It took effect on August 1, 2009.[99] The formula used for calculating benefits under this program is different than the "set rate" used by the MGIB-AD, MGIB-SR and REAP programs. Instead, the maximum benefit is linked to each individual's "subsistence, tuition, fees, and other educational costs" while participating in an approved program of education.[100] In general, reservists who have been activated since September 11, 2001, will receive a significantly greater benefit under the Post-9/11 GI Bill than under MGIB-SR, MGIB-AD, or REAP. However, there are some circumstances in which it would be more beneficial for the reservist to elect to use one of these latter educational assistance programs. Another key difference between the Post-9/11 GI Bill and REAP is that the former is based on aggregate time served on active duty since September 11th, while the latter is based on the longest consecutive period of active duty performed since September 11th unless the aggregate service is at least three years.

The maximum benefit under this law is provided to (1) individuals who have served at least 36 aggregate months on active duty in the Armed Forces after September 10, 2001, and who subsequently continue to serve or who are discharged or released from service under specified conditions;[101] and (2) individuals who have served at least 30 continuous days of active duty after September 10, 2001, and who are discharged or released from active duty for a service-connected disability. For reserve component personnel, the law defines "active duty" as service under six specific activation authorities of Title 10, two additional types of service by National Guard personnel under Title 32, and one additional type of service by Coast Guard reservists.[102]

---

[98] P.L. 110-181, National Defense Authorization Act for Fiscal Year 2008, Section 530, January 28, 2008. Additionally, as part of the original language, those involuntarily separated from the Selected Reserve, Individual Ready Reserve or Inactive National Guard on account of disability have 10 years to use the benefit.

[99] For more information on this program, see CRS Report R42755, *The Post-9/11 Veterans Educational Assistance Act of 2008 (Post-9/11 GI Bill): Primer and Issues*, by Cassandria Dortch.

[100] 38 U.S.C. §3313(a).

[101] The following types of discharge or release from active duty qualify: (1) an honorable discharge from active duty; (2) a release after service on active duty, characterized as honorable, for placement on "the retired list, transfer to the Fleet Reserve or Fleet Marine Corps Reserve, or placement on the temporary disability retired list"; (3) a release from active duty, characterized as honorable, for further service in a reserve component; and (4) a discharge or release from active duty, characterized as honorable, due to a pre-existing medical condition, hardship, or a physical or mental condition which interfered with the individual's performance of duty but which was not characterized as a disability and was not the result of willful misconduct. 38 U.S.C. §3311(c).

[102] As initially passed, the Post-9/11 GI Bill defined "active duty" for members of the reserve components as "service on active duty under a call or order to active duty under Section 688, 12301(a), 12301(d), 12301(g), 12302 or 12304 of Title 10." These are the authorities most commonly used to activate members of the National Guard and Reserve for overseas military operations, such as the ongoing operations in Afghanistan, as well as for certain domestic military (continued...)

A reduced benefit is available to individuals who have served at least 90 aggregate days, but less than 36 aggregate months. This reduced benefit is scaled so that those serving longer aggregate periods of time on active duty receive a higher benefit than those serving shorter aggregate periods of times.[103]

The amount of the educational assistance benefit has three major components. The first provides a payment to cover "the actual net cost for in-State tuition and fees" for public institutions of higher learning, and up to $19,198.31 per year for nonpublic or foreign institutions.[104] This amount is reduced by waivers or reductions of tuition and fees, and by certain types of scholarships and student aid.[105] The second major component provides a monthly housing stipend equal to the Basic Allowance for Housing which an active duty servicemember in paygrade E-5, with dependents, would receive if living in the area where the institution of higher learning is located.[106] The third component provides a payment equivalent to $1,000 per academic year to cover "books, supplies, equipment and other educational costs."[107]

(...continued)

operations such as Operation Noble Eagle. However, in addition to these authorities, members of the National Guard frequently serve on duty full-time under Title 32. The two most common circumstances for this type of duty are (1) full-time National Guard duty under 32 U.S.C. 502(f) for service in the Active Guard and Reserve program, and (2) full-time National Guard duty under 32 U.S.C. 502(f) for service in support of domestic emergencies, such as the airport security mission performed immediately after the September 11th attacks, the response to hurricanes Katrina and Rita, and the southwest border security mission. This duty did not count as qualifying service for the purposes of the original Post-9/11 GI Bill, as it was not included in the law's definition of "active duty." However, this was changed in the 111th Congress. P.L. 111-377, the Post-9/11 Veterans Educational Assistance Improvements Act of 2010, added as qualifying duty both full-time National Guard duty "for the purpose of organizing, administering, recruiting, instructing, or training the National Guard" (that is, service in the Active Guard and Reserve program), and service under 32 U.S.C. 502(f) "when authorized by the President or Secretary of Defense for the purpose of responding to a national emergency declared by the President and supported by federal funds." For more information on these changes, see CRS Report R41620, *The Post-9/11 Veterans Educational Assistance Improvements Act of 2010, As Enacted*, by Cassandria Dortch. Finally, the National Defense Authorization Act for FY2013 (P.L. 112-239, sec. 681(c)) added activation of Coast Guard reservists under 14 U.S.C. 712 as a qualifying type of active duty. Note that the new activation authorities (12304a, Disaster Response Activation; 12304b, Combatant Command Support Activation) are not included in the definition of active duty for purposes of the Post-9/11 GI Bill.

[103] The proportion of the maximum benefit for service less than 36 months is as follows: 90% of the maximum benefit for those who serve an aggregate of at least 30 months, but less than 36 months, including service in entry level and skill training; 80% of the maximum benefit for those who serve an aggregate of at least 24 months, but less than 30 months, including service in entry level and skill training; 70% of the maximum benefit for those who serve an aggregate of at least 18 months, but less than 24 months, excluding entry level and skill training; 60% of the maximum benefit for those who serve an aggregate of at least 12 months, but less than 18 months, excluding entry level and skill training; 50% of the maximum benefit for those who serve an aggregate of at least 6 months, but less than 12 months, excluding entry level and skill training; 40% of the maximum benefit for those who serve an aggregate of at least 90 days, but less than 6 months, excluding entry level and skill training. Note that entry level and skill training is counted for aggregate service of 24 months or more; it is excluded for aggregate service of less than 24 months. 38 U.S.C. 3311(c).

[104]38 U.S.C. 3313(c)(1)(A). However, the Restoring GI Bill Fairness Act (P.L. 112-26) allows certain individuals to more than this maximum for tuition and fees. See CRS Report R42755, *The Post-9/11 Veterans Educational Assistance Act of 2008 (Post-9/11 GI Bill): Primer and Issues*, by Cassandria Dortch.

[105] 38 U.S.C. §3313(c)(1)(A).

[106] 38 U.S.C. §3313(c)(1)(B)(i). Based on 2014 rates for the Basic Allowance for Housing, this stipend could range from $840 to $3,744 per month. Individuals pursing their studies more than half-time but less than full-time will have this stipend proportionally reduced. Individuals pursuing their studies on a half-time basis or less do not qualify for this stipend. See 38 U.S.C. §3313(f). Individuals still on active duty are not eligible for this stipend. See 38 U.S.C. §3313(e). Individuals pursuing "a program of education solely through distance learning on more than a half-time basis" are eligible for a stipend worth half of the amount of the normal stipend. See 38 U.S.C. §3313(c)(1)(B)(iii). Individuals using their benefit for apprenticeship or on the job training have their housing calculated based on the (continued...)

In addition to the educational assistance benefit, the Post-9/11 GI Bill may also provide a tutorial assistance benefit of up to $100 per month (not to exceed $1,200 total), a one-time relocation and travel assistance payment of $500, a payment of up to $2,000 for each licensure and certification test, and a payment to cover the cost of a national test to gain admission to, or course credit at, an institution of higher learning.[108] Other provisions of the bill allow for enhanced benefits for servicemembers with critical skills or who perform additional service, and for servicemembers attending schools which have entered into a matching contribution program known as the "Yellow Ribbon G.I. Education Enhancement Program."[109] Finally, the bill allows eligible servicemembers to transfer some or all of their benefits to a spouse and children.[110]

Financial Losses for Some Mobilized Reservists

The mobilization of reservists in the aftermath of the September 11, 2001, terrorist attacks has been the largest since at least the Korean War and one of the longest ongoing mobilizations ever.[111] Some of these reservists have experienced financial losses when moving from their civilian jobs to full time military status. These losses occur due to differences between the reservists' military and civilian pay, expenses incurred by reservists because of mobilization, and the decline in business experienced by self-employed reservists during and after release from active duty. This has generated numerous complaints from mobilized reservists and helped generate congressional interest in the subject.

Income Replacement for Certain Reserve Component Personnel

The 109th Congress enacted a provision that provides a special payment of up to $3,000 to certain reservists who experience income loss while involuntarily mobilized.[112] Reservists who have

---

(...continued)

location of the employer. See §3313(g)(3)(B)(i).

[107] 38 U.S.C. §3313(c)(1)(B)(iv). Individuals pursuing their studies on a half-time basis or less will have this stipend proportionally reduced. See 38 U.S.C. §3313(f). Individuals pursuing programs of education in pursuit of a certificate or other non-college degree will receive a stipend of up to $83 per month. See 38 U.S.C. §3313(g)(3)(A). Individuals pursuing a full-time program of apprenticeship or other on-job training will receive a stipend of up to $83 per month. See 38 U.S.C. §3313(g)(3)(B). Individuals enrolled in a program of education consisting of flight training or a program of education pursued exclusively by correspondence are not eligible for the stipend. See 38 U.S.C. §3313(g)(3)(C and D).

[108] 38 U.S.C. §3314, 3318, 3315, and 3315A, respectively.

[109] 38 U.S.C. §3316 & 3317, respectively.

[110] 38 U.S.C. §3319. There is an additional provision, known as the Marine Gunnery Sergeant John David Fry Scholarship, that provides benefits to the children of individuals who die in the line of duty while serving on active duty. 38 U.S.C. §3311(b)(9) and (f).

[111] Given the lack of clarity on the methodology used to count activated reservists in the Korean War, especially with respect to how volunteers were counted, it is unclear whether or not the post-9/11 call up has been larger than the Korean War call up. If only involuntary activations are included, it is probable that Korean War callup is still larger than the post-9/11 callup; however, if voluntary activations are included, the reverse is probably true. The mobilization in the aftermath of September 11, 2001, has been underway for over 12 years. The mobilization in support of the Kosovo mission, though much smaller in size, began in May 1999 and is still ongoing (15 years). By comparison, the World War II mobilization lasted from August 1940 to early 1946 (approximately 5 ½ years), while the Korean War mobilization lasted from July 1950 to December 1953 (approximately 3 ½ years).

[112] P.L. 109-163, National Defense Authorization Act for FY2006, Section 614, January 6, 2006, codified at 37 U.S.C. 910. Payments under this provision may also be made to individuals who meet the definition of extended or frequent mobilization, as well as those who are "retained on active duty under subparagraph (A) or (B) of Section 12301(h)(1) (continued...)

---

experienced income loss become eligible for these payments in every full month of active duty *following the month in which they* (1) complete 18 consecutive months of active duty under an involuntary mobilization order; (2) complete 24 months of active duty under an involuntary mobilization order out of the previous 60 months; or (3) are involuntarily mobilized for a period of 180 days or more within six months or less of a previous period of involuntary active duty for a period of 180 days or more. The amount of compensation available under this provision is equal to the reservist's "average monthly civilian income" minus "total monthly military compensation."[113] However, the amount may not be less than $50 per month or more than $3,000 per month. Involuntary activations of National Guard personnel under 32 U.S.C. 502(f)(1)—the section of law commonly used for domestic emergency response—do count as qualifying duty for the purposes of this payment.[114]

Differential Pay for Mobilized Federal Employees

The 111th Congress enacted a provision, codified at 5 U.S.C. 5538, to minimize the income loss of civilian employees of the federal government who are involuntarily[115] ordered to active duty or involuntarily retained on active duty.[116] It does so by providing "differential pay"—a payment

---

(...continued)

of Title 10 because of an injury or illness incurred or aggravated while the member was assigned to duty in an area for which special pay under Section 310 [Special Pay for Duty Subject to Hostile Fire or Imminent Danger] of this title is available." The statutory language does not define the term "involuntary mobilization," but the regulations promulgated by the Department of Defense define it as "an order to duty under Title 10 United States Code, (U.S.C.), 12301(a), 12301(g), 12302, or 12304, without the consent of the member or order to full-time National Guard duty under 32 U.S.C. 502(f)(1)." See Department of Defense Financial Management Regulation (FMR) 7000.14-R, Volume 7A, Chapter 55, paragraph 550203, available at http://comptroller.defense.gov/fmr/current/07a/Volume_07a.pdf . Note that duty under the two new activation authorities (12304a, Disaster Response Activation; 12304b, Combatant Command Support Activation) are not included in the definition of involuntary mobilization. This may simply be because the relevant section of the FRM has not been updated since June 2012, prior to enactment of the new authorities.

[113] The term "average monthly civilian income" means "the amount, determined by the Secretary concerned, of the earned income of the member for either the 12 months preceding the member's mobilization or the 12 months covered by the member's most recent Federal income tax filing, divided by 12." The term "total monthly military compensation" means "the amount, computed on a monthly basis, of the sum of—(A) the amount of regular military compensation (RMC); and (B) any amount of special pay or incentive pay and any allowance (other than an allowance included in regular military compensation) that is paid to the member on a monthly basis." Regular military compensation (RMC) is defined in 37 U.S.C. 101(25) as "the total of the following elements that a member of a uniformed service accrues or receives, directly or indirectly, in cash or in kind every payday: basic pay, basic allowance for housing, basic allowance for subsistence, and Federal tax advantage accruing to the aforementioned allowances because they are not subject to Federal income tax."

[114] See footnote 112.

[115] The law specifies that in order to be eligible for differential pay, the individual must be "absent from a position of employment with the Federal Government in order to perform active duty in the uniformed services pursuant to a call or order to active duty under a provision of law referred to in Section 101(a)(13)(B) of Title 10." The provisions of law referred to in Section 101(a)(13)(B) of Title 10 are Sections 688, 12301(a), 12302, 12304, 12304a, 12305, and 12406, and Chapter 15, all of which are involuntary activation or retention authorities (that is, they do not require the consent of the member to be used). The definition in Section 101(a)(13)(B) also makes reference to "any other provision of law during a war or during a national emergency declared by the President or Congress," but it does not appear from the legislative history that this was intended to extend the provision beyond the specific authorities mentioned. As such, the OPM implementation guidance (see footnote 117) defines qualifying duty as duty under one of the specified authorities. However, the OPM guidance was drafted in 2011, prior to enactment of 10 U.S.C. 12304a (Disaster Response Activation), so it does not yet reference this new activation authority. 10 U.S.C. 12304b was not included in the definition of 10 U.S.C. 101(a)(13)(B), so duty under this new authority, were it to be used, would not qualify.

[116] P.L. 111-8, Omnibus Appropriations Act, 2009, Section 751, March 11, 2009; amended by P.L. 111-117, Consolidated Appropriations Act, 2010, Section 745, December 16, 2009.

---

equal to the amount by which a reservist's military pay and allowances are lower than his or her civilian basic pay. Specific eligibility criteria and the method for calculating the amount of differential pay are outlined in a memorandum issued by the Office of Personnel Management.[117] This provision only applies to federal government employees, but it is not limited to cases of extended or frequent activations like the Income Replacement provision discussed in the previous paragraph. Full-time National Guard duty under Title 32 does not count as qualifying duty for the purposes of this payment.

Reducing the Age at Which Certain Reservists Can Draw Retired Pay

After completing 20 years of qualifying service, a reservist may apply for retirement. Once retired, the reservist is entitled to receive certain benefits immediately; however, until recently he or she was not entitled to receive retired pay until the age of 60. In light of the heavy use of the Reserve Component in recent years, a number of legislative proposals were introduced in the 108th and 109th Congresses to lower the age at which reservists receive retired pay and military retiree health care benefits. During the 110th Congress, a provision was included in the National Defense Authorization Act for FY2008 which permits certain reservists to draw retired pay as early as age 50, while maintaining the age for access to the military health care system at 60.[118]

This provision reduced the age for receipt of retired pay for members of the Ready Reserve by three months for each aggregate of 90 days of specified duty performed in any fiscal year after January 28, 2008 (the date of enactment of the FY2008 National Defense Authorization Act). Specified duty includes active duty under any provision of law referred to in 10 U.S.C. 101(a)(13)(B), active duty under 10 U.S.C. 12301(d); or active service under 32 U.S.C. 502(f) if responding to a national emergency declared by the President or supported by federal funds.[119] The retired pay eligibility age cannot be reduced below age 50, and eligibility for retiree health care benefits remains at age 60. This law has no effect on: reservists who were already retired as of January 28, 2008; reservists who do not perform any of the types of specified duty during their careers; or reservists who only performed the specified duty prior to January 28, 2008. It only reduces the retirement age for those reservists who perform qualifying duty after January 28, 2008.

Section 660 of the Senate version of the National Defense Authorization Act for FY2010 would have included service performed between September 11, 2001, and January 28, 2008, as

---

[117] Office of Personnel Management, *OPM Policy Guidance Regarding Reservist Differential Under 5 U.S.C. 5538*, date April 11, 2011, available at http://www.opm.gov/policy-data-oversight/pay-leave/pay-administration/reservist-differential/policyguidance.pdf.

[118] 10 U.S.C. 12731(f).

[119] See footnote 115 for the provisions of law referred to in 10 U.S.C. 101(a)(13)(B). Qualifying duty includes mobilization in support of Operation Noble Eagle, Enduring Freedom, or Iraqi Freedom/New Dawn, provided the duty occurs after January 28, 2008. It also includes National Guard duty under 32 U.S.C. 502(f), provided it occurs after January 28, 2008, and is in response to a national emergency declared by the President or a national emergency supported by federal funds. Active Guard and Reserve duty organizing, administering, recruiting, instructing, or training the reserve component does not qualify. One of the new activation authorities (10 U.S.C. 12304a, Disaster Response Activation) was included in 10 U.S.C. 101(a)(13)(B), so duty performed under this authority can qualify for early retirement credit provided the other requirements for qualification are met. The other new activation authority (10 U.S.C. 12304b, Combatant Command Support Activation) was not included in the definition of 10 U.S.C. 101(a)(13)(B), so duty under this new authority, were it to be used, would not qualify

---

qualifying service for the purpose of lowering the age at which a reservist can draw retired pay. However, there was no corresponding provision in the House version, and it was not included in the final bill.[120] The conference report which accompanied the final bill stated: "the conferees would support the provision provided that acceptable offsets are identified consistent with budgetary requirements of both the Senate and the House of Representatives."[121]

Author Contact Information

Lawrence Kapp

Specialist in Military Manpower Policy
lkapp@crs.loc.gov, 7-7609

Barbara Salazar Torreon

Information Research Specialist
btorreon@crs.loc.gov, 7-8996

---

[120] P.L. 111-84.

[121] U.S. Congress, House Committee on Armed Services, *National Defense Authorization Act for Fiscal Year 2010*, Conference Report to Accompany H.R. 2647, 111th Cong., 1st sess., October 7, 2009, H.Rept. 111-288 (Washington: GPO, 2009), p. 767.

www.ingramcontent.com/pod-product-compliance
Lightning Source LLC
Chambersburg PA
CBHW052023280526
45793CB00005B/1106